PORTRAIT OF
SOUTHAMPTON

Adam Burton

HALSGROVE

First published in Great Britain in 2009

British Library Cataloguing-in-Publication Data
A CIP record for this title is available from the British Library

ISBN 978 1 84114 871 7

HALSGROVE
Halsgrove House,
Ryelands Industrial Estate,
Bagley Road, Wellington, Somerset TA21 9PZ
Tel: 01823 653777   Fax: 01823 216796
email: sales@halsgrove.com

Part of the Halsgrove group of companies
Information on all Halsgrove titles is available at: www.halsgrove.com

Printed and bound by Grafiche Flaminia, Italy

Introduction

A brief history of Southampton

Southampton is one of the largest cities on the South Coast of England, and for many years has been a major port. Its strong links to the sea have featured prominently in its shaping into the modern city we see today.

With a history of habitation stretching back to the stone age, the first substantial settlement was founded by the Romans in AD 43 shortly after the invasion of Britain. Situated in what is now Bitterne Manor, Clausentum was a large trading settlement for the Romans, and was occupied until around 410.

After the decline of the Roman Empire, the Anglo Saxons created a new larger settlement on the opposite side of the Itchen River named Hamwic. In the tenth century the settlement again moved to the present site of modern day Southampton. As the medieval town grew in size and population, its name first evolved into Hamtun, and subsequently Hampton.

After the Norman Conquest in 1066, Southampton rose to prominence as a busy port. With its close proximity to Winchester, it became a key link in the trading chain between the old English capital and Normandy. By the thirteenth century Southampton had become a major port, trading French Wine in return for English cloth and wool.

The town became prosperous through its trading links and fine merchant houses sprang up near the quayside. But in the Hundred Years War, Southampton paid a heavy price for its privileged coastal location, when the old town was sacked by a French raiding party in 1338. Having no walls to defend the town, the invaders murdered its inhabitants and looted its possessions. Shortly afterwards, King Edward III ordered major defensive walls to be built to protect Southampton from future attacks. Many of these fortifications are still standing today, particularly along the West Quay.

It was from West Quay, in 1620 that the Pilgrim Fathers boarded the Mayflower and Speedwell for their voyage to America. Southampton's importance as a port has made it central to many departures throughout the years, particularly for military operations. The armies of Henry V departed from Southampton en route to the Battle of Agincourt in 1415. Countless troops have passed through the port to fight in the Crimean War, the Boer War and both World Wars.

In the nineteenth century Southampton's maritime connections took another huge leap forward. The creation of the Docks coincided with the opening of a direct rail link to London, making Southampton the number one UK port for passengers departing on transatlantic liners. Where the port of Liverpool had previously been known as *Gateway to the Empire* Southampton now became *Gateway to the World*.

As Southampton became synonymous with transatlantic cruising, many of the richest people in the world passed through the town, to board some of the most luxurious ships ever built. Such iconic ships as the *Mauritania*, *Queen Mary* and *QE2* to name but a few, have all had Southampton as their home port.

But no ship could be more infamous than the RMS *Titanic*, which sailed from Southampton on its maiden voyage on 12 April 1912. Southampton will always remain closely linked with the tragic story of the *Titanic*. Many hundreds of the crew who perished were Sotonians, their legacies are remembered in memorials and gravestones all over the city.

As the docks continued to grow in prominence, Southampton became a key target for enemy attack during the Second World War. Much of the town was destroyed from enemy bombing throughout the war, including many historical buildings. One of the biggest targets was the Supermarine Aviation Works in Woolston; it was here that R J Mitchell designed arguably the most famous and iconic aeroplane in British history, the Spitfire.

A major rebuilding campaign followed the Second World War and reshaped the town centre. Over the years, this trend has continued as buildings have been replaced with modern new designs, while careful attention has been given to preserving the historical buildings of the old town.

In 1964 Southampton's importance was again recognised as it gained City status. Being one of the younger cities, it constantly strives to compete in an industrious and ever-changing modern world. Retaining its maritime connections, Southampton continues to be the UK's number one port for international cruise ships, and the rejuvenation of this industry has been embraced wholeheartedly in the city. In addition the docks now contain the UK's second largest container port, transporting supplies all over the world.

This same level of success can be witnessed throughout the city; Southampton is now the premier retail city on the South Coast; its University and Oceanography Centre is widely respected throughout the world, its airport is the fastest growing major airport in Europe.

These are all signs that modern day Southampton is matching the legacy of its illustrious past to provide its inhabitants with an exciting city for the future.

Adam Burton

Finished in 1939, the impressive Southampton Civic Centre houses not only the council offices, but also an art gallery, library, police station and guildhall. Pictured here is the south wing, which is occupied by Southampton City Council.

The distinctive Civic Centre clock tower, reflected in the modern glass-fronted BBC South studios.

The Civic Centre clock tower is a distinctive structure of the Southampton skyline. It was once known as Kimbers Chimney, after the former city mayor Sidney Kimber.

Left:
Opened in 1933 the Civic Centre west wing housed the city's law courts. After these were eventually relocated to London Road, the building became, and still remains the Central Police Station.

Opened in 1939, the north wing hosts both the Southampton Art Gallery and Library. The gallery is internationally renowned for its impressive art collection, which includes over 3500 pieces covering six centuries of European art history.

This fountain was initially positioned in the Rose Garden on the opposite side of the Civic Centre. It was moved to its present position outside the gallery when the Rose Garden was removed to make way for a major road intersection.

Late afternoon on an autumnal day outside the Art Gallery.

Early summer morning sunshine lights up the beautiful north wing entrance of the Civic Centre buildings.

Elaborate sea creatures adorn the lamp posts outside the central
police station giving a sense of Southampton's coastal location.

Opened in 2000, WestQuay elevated Southampton to be the premier shopping destination on the South Coast. The 33 acre site contains over 100 shops.

Sweeping curves of modern architecture at Arundel Circus, a major entrance to WestQuay shopping centre. The glass tower was designed to bear resemblance to the ancient castle defence Arundel Tower, which stands close by.

This modern footbridge spanning the busy Castle Way road follows the path of the old town walls.

The modern design at WestQuay is a beautiful example of the use of glass in contemporary architecture.

Southampton's past and present are never more apparent than where the old town walls meet WestQuay.

Right:
Arundel Tower stands at the northwest boundary of the medieval town of Southampton.

Replica footsteps near Catchcold Tower form part of the 'Walk the Southampton Walls' experience.

Built in the early 1400s Prince Edward Tower is a prominent feature in the medieval west walls. It is also known as Catchcold Tower, presumably due to its once exposed location beside the River Test.

Sadly, Southampton castle no longer remains, but evidence of its location can be seen at the Castle Watergate. Built into the heavily fortified west walls in the fourteenth century the Castle Watergate and quay provided direct access for the transportation of wine from ships to the castle vaults.

Another example of Southampton's past and present living side by side. This archway connects the medieval walls with St Michael's Church via modern residential buildings.

At first glance this reconstruction of a medieval merchant
boat beside Western Esplanade seems strangely out of place,
landlocked and close to a busy road. Yet, it helps to visualise a time
when the coastal waters lapped close to the walls of the old town.
In medieval Southampton, this area formed the West Quay.

Right:
Some of the finest preserved and most unique fortifications lie
on the western edge of the old town. These arched defences,
known as The Arcades, were initially the walls of houses
that were subsequently fortified to guard against French
invasion during the 100 Years War.

Modern illuminations ensure that The Arcades remain a prominent feature of present day Southampton.

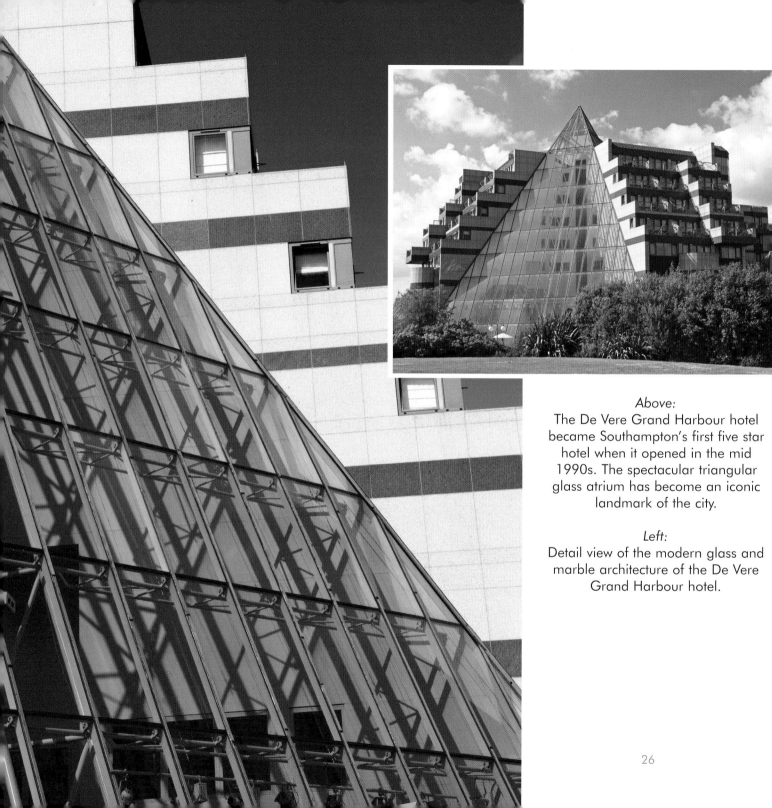

Above:
The De Vere Grand Harbour hotel became Southampton's first five star hotel when it opened in the mid 1990s. The spectacular triangular glass atrium has become an iconic landmark of the city.

Left:
Detail view of the modern glass and marble architecture of the De Vere Grand Harbour hotel.

Established in 1968, the Southampton Boat Show is one of the city's most prestigious annual events. In this image, a magnificent Sunseeker motor cruiser is on display outside the Grand Harbour hotel.

The Westgate provided access to the West Quay for loading and unloading of goods from the many merchant ships visiting the old town. Through this archway in 1415 Henry V's armies marched en route to the Battle of Agincourt.

The Tudor Merchants Hall stands beside the Westgate in Westgate Street.

City viewpoint from the top of The Arcades on the western fringe of the old town.

Close to this memorial on the old West Quay in 1620 the Pilgrim Fathers embarked on their journey to America in the *Mayflower* and the *Speedwell*. Due to the condition of the *Speedwell*, the ships stopped again at Plymouth, before the *Mayflower* eventually set sail alone to the new world.

Signpost indicating the route of 'Walk the Southampton Walls' the self guided tour of the old town.

The white building on the left was once the Royal Southern Yacht Club. Built in 1846 in stuccoed Italianate Classical style it was among the finest Victorian buildings in the city. To the right, the Wool House was built in the fourteenth century as a warehouse. Once used to hold French prisoners during the Napoleonic War, it is now home to the Maritime Museum.

La Regata is a popular family-run Spanish restaurant located opposite Town Quay.

Opened in 1930 and recently restored to its former glory, the Royal Pier gatehouse stands proudly at the head of the pier. Unfortunately, the pier itself has fallen into disrepair and has been closed to the public since 1982.

Thanks to the efforts of local restaurant business Kuti's, this iconic Southampton building has once again reopened to the public. Its transformation to Kuti's Royal Thai Pier was completed when the restaurant formerly opened its doors for the first time in the summer of 2008.

The old Harbour Master's Building adds a sense of historical grandness to Town Quay.

Now redeveloped as Maxim Casino, the old Harbour Master's Building is beautifully illuminated at night.

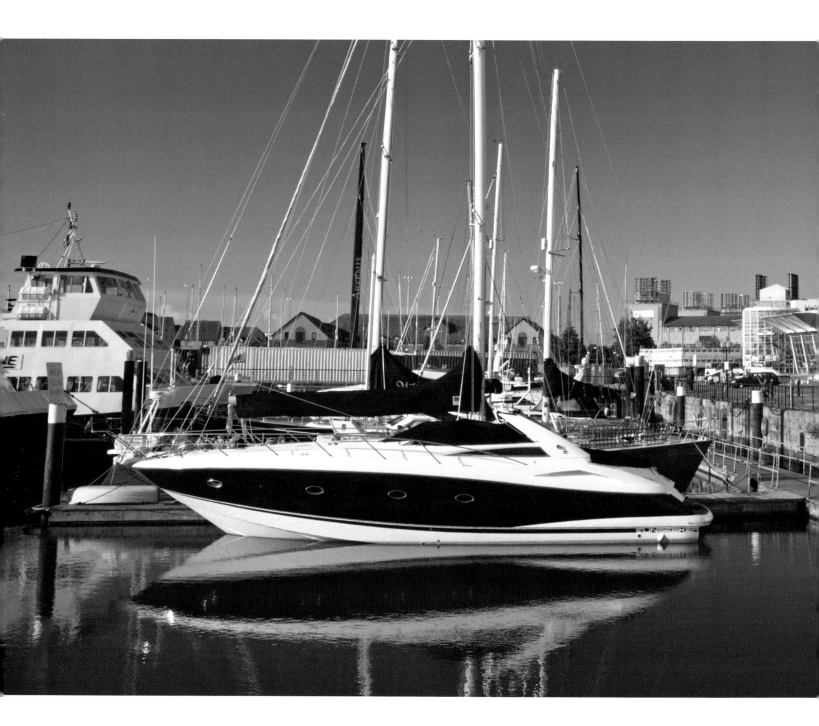

Historically used to guide ships safely into Southampton Water, the Calshot Spit lightship has been permanently secured at Ocean Village since 1988.

Left:
Once part of Southampton Docks, Ocean Village Marina is now a hotspot for private yachts and luxury motor cruisers.

S ᐁ R

THIS TABLET IS ERECTED IN
MEMORY OF THOSE WHO FELL
IN THE 1939 – 1945 WAR

DOCKS &   MARINE

BAGLEY W. H.	MAULE H.
BARKER J. W.	MEARS D.
ENYON J.	MILLS L.
BLIGH R. N.	PARSONS J. A.
BROOKER S.	POINTER J.
BROWN J.	REEVES T.
CHAMBERS M. H.	ROSS C.
CHARLTON H. F. D.	SIMMONS W. F.
COLLINGS K. V. G.	STANSBRIDGE E.
DAGNELL E. C.	STARK A.
FALLOON J.	STEPHENS A. C. W.
FISHER R. F.	TANNER E. E.
GORDON A.	WARD A. E. (MRS)
GORDON R. A.	WEBB E.
HAWES R. W.	WEBB W. C. F.
HAWKES J. W.	WEEKES H.
HELLYAR A.	WHITE A. G. S.
HENRY W. R.	WILSON W.
IRELAND B.	WRIGHT E.
LAVERICK K. W.	YORK F. C.
LONGMAN W.	YOUNG C. A.
LUSH L.	

"THEIR NAME LIVETH FOR EVERMORE"

1939   1945

Tablet on the wall of the Ferry House building in Ocean Village, commemorating dockworkers that lost their lives in the Second World War.

Now empty office space, Canute Chambers hides a poignant history. This building was once the Southampton headquarters of White Star Line. In 1912, after the sinking of the ill-fated RMS *Titanic*, crowds gathered here desperate for news of whether their loved ones had survived.

Buildings at the entrance to Ocean Village Marina.

Embedded in the pedestrian paving at Ocean Village, this mast is symbolic of the area's maritime past and present.

Left:
Looking across Ocean Village Marina to modern residential apartments.

Luxurious boats moored in Ocean Village
Marina in the summertime.

Right:
Tranquil evening overlooking the many
moored boats at Ocean Village Marina.

Modern yachts moored side by side in Ocean Village Marina.

Yachts moored opposite the Royal Southampton Yacht Club building in Ocean Village Marina.

Opened in 1995, Harbour Lights offers an alternative to multiplex cinemas, and screens a wide range of films from arthouse and world cinema to Hollywood blockbusters.

The unusual building, designed by architects Burrell Foley Fischer, is a striking structure on the Ocean Village waterfront.

Ocean car-park is Southampton's newest multi-storey car-park. The modern structure has been shortlisted for several design awards, and provides the first phase of the £70m project to redevelop Ocean Village.

Many organisations have large office buildings along Maritime Walk, some overlooking the Ocean Village Marina.

Modern office buildings near Ocean Way.

Residential accommodation is in demand at Ocean Village. Many of the apartments have views over the marina or, as pictured here, views over Southampton Water.

The William Chamberlayne
Gas Column in Houndwell
Park has been relocated on
no less than four occasions
since it was originally
unveiled in the early
nineteenth century.

The City of Southampton Arms engraved on the
William Chamberlayne Gas Column.

Early autumn in Andrews Park. The park was named in honour of Richard Andrews (1796 – 1859), five times the mayor of Southampton and owner of a coach-building business in Above Bar.

The remains of Holy Rood Church on the High Street.

On 30 November 1940 Holy Rood Church was destroyed by enemy bombing during the Second World War. Its ruins have been preserved by the people of Southampton as a memorial and garden of rest.

Known as the Church of the Sailors, the ruins of Holy Rood provide a memorial to merchant seamen lost at sea. Inside these gates stands a memorial to the crew of the *Titanic*.

The grand façade of
an old bank building
on the High Street.

A quiet summer morning on Bugle Street beside St Michael's Square, with the
Tudor House museum on the left overhanging the pavement.

Above:
Evening descends on St Michael's Square, with the Tudor House being atmospherically illuminated by the mock antique style streetlights.

Left:
Built in the fifteenth century, Tudor House museum is one of Southampton's most recognisable historical buildings. In recent years it has been closed to the public while it has undergone major restoration.

Right:
Tudor House was once owned by Sir Richard Lyster, Lord Chief Justice of England. During this time King Henry VIII stayed here with Anne Boleyn. It is rumoured that the ghost of the ill fated queen still haunts the house.

Below:
Originally built for Sir John Dawtry, the Controller of Customs in Southampton, Tudor House has been a family home, an artist's studio and has also housed businesses including a dye-house and a bookbinder.

Built in 1070, St Michael's Church is thought to be the oldest building in Southampton. The church is sandwiched between Bugle Street and Castle Way.

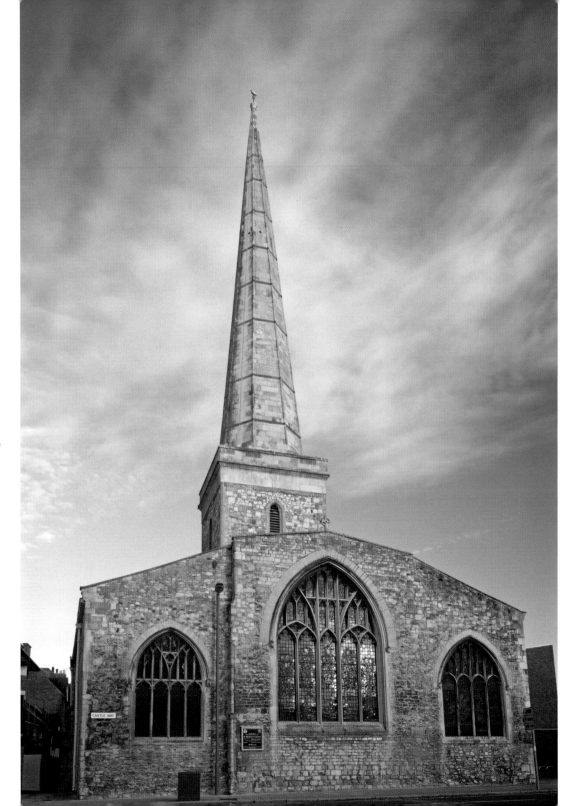

On Sunday 4 October 1338 during the 100 Years War, a fleet of 50 French galleys landed at West Quay. A French raiding party broke into St Michael's Church, slaying many townspeople who were at mass.

Situated on French Street, this fourteenth century building is one of the earliest surviving medieval merchant's houses in England. It was built as both a place of business and home for merchant John Fortin, who like many others in Southampton would have traded wine and other goods with European ports.

Right:
The magnificent Bargate is the iconic building of Southampton. Once the main gateway to the old walled town, it is now preserved as a lasting monument to Southampton's prestigious heritage.

The two lions which guard the entrance to the Bargate reflect the legendry exploits of Sir Bevis of Hampton. The original wooden statues were erected in 1522 to commemorate the visit of King Charles V of Spain. They were replaced in 1743 with the present lead statues.

Left:
The heavily fortified north face of the Bargate presented an imposing structure to all entering the old town. Initially, the gatehouse consisted of a simple square tower and archway. Between the thirteenth and fifteenth centuries, various additions were made, completing the familiar structure we know today.

While it is now isolated amongst modern retail buildings, the ancient Bargate still outshines all other structures in the city centre.

Right:
On the south face of the Bargate a statue of George III in Roman dress overlooks the High Street. On the inside of the three arched windows lies the hall, which used to be the town's courtroom.

An unusual sight in the city centre; the High Street precinct is deserted on an early summer morning.

Once Southampton's prime retail location, Above Bar precinct is still a popular shopping area. The wide overhang visible on the left is the main entrance into WestQuay shopping centre.

At the time of its opening WestQuay was the biggest inner-city shopping centre development in the UK. Viewed here from Harbour Parade, the huge complex has regalvanised retail in the city.

A modern glass framed elevator ascends behind the tinted façade of WestQuay shopping centre.

The John Lewis department store at WestQuay is one of the largest outside of London. It is double the size of the store it superseded, the long established and respected Southampton store Tyrrell & Green. Although taken over by the John Lewis Partnership in 1934, it was not until the store's move to WestQuay in 2000 that it finally changed name to John Lewis.

Early autumn evening beside the
'Enclosure' sculpture in Watts Park.

Right:
This Portland stone sculpture in
Watts Park, entitled 'Enclosure' was commissioned
in 2000 under the Heritage Lottery Scheme as
part of a £4.5m refurbishment of Southampton's central
parks. It was created by artist Paul De Monchaux.

This elaborate statue in Watts Park commemorates one of the city's most famous sons. Born in Southampton, Isaac Watts (1674–1748) was the first prolific and popular English hymn writer. He wrote over 750 hymns and is remembered as the 'Father of English Hymnody'.

Due to its many central parks which cover over 1100 hectares in the city centre, Southampton has earned the title of 'the Green City'. The Civic Centre clock tower can be seen here above the trees of Watts Park.

A cyclist commuting home from work through the leafy paths of Watts Park.

At the top of Above Bar Street, the Cenotaph has stood since 1920. Designed by renowned British architect Sir Edwin Lutyens, the Cenotaph is the city's major memorial to remember those who fell in war.

Left:
The grand entrance to the Southampton Guildhall, the south's largest multi purpose entertainment venue. The Guildhall's size makes it the perfect venue to hold large social events and live music performances.

GREATER LOVE HATH NO MAN THAN
THIS, THAT A MAN LAY DOWN HIS
LIFE FOR HIS FRIENDS.
ST JOHN 15TH CH. 13TH V

TO THE MEMORY OF THE ENGINEER OFFICERS
OF THE R.M.S. "TITANIC" WHO SHOWED
THEIR HIGH CONCEPTION OF DUTY AND THEIR
HEROISM BY REMAINING AT THEIR POSTS
15TH APRIL 1912.

The *Titanic* memorial in Andrews Park was unveiled in 1914 in front of nearly 100,000 people. It commemorates the engineers who lost their lives on the ill-fated ship in 1912, most of whom were from Southampton.

Right:
There are many stories of heroic deeds that surround the sinking of the *Titanic*; one of the most famous was that of the engineers. Despite their fates being sealed with the sinking ship, they worked tirelessly to keep the lights burning brightly until moments before she sank.

GREATER LOVE HATH NO MAN THAN
THIS, THAT A MAN LAY DOWN HIS
LIFE FOR HIS FRIENDS.
ST JOHN 15TH CH. 13TH V.

Bedford Place is a busy area to the north of the city centre offering many different independent shops, restaurants and nightlife.

Early summer morning at an unusually deserted Bedford Place.

The fine Georgian buildings lining Carlton Crescent bear witness to a prestigious residential history for this area of Southampton.

Modern apartment blocks in the Polygon mark the site of the old Polygon Hotel. One of Southampton's most famous hotels, the Polygon played its part in two world wars. In the Great War, the headquarters of the British Expeditionary Force camped in the hotel, while in the Second World War it was the headquarters for the 14th Major Port US army in the lead up to the D-Day invasion.

Memorial stone in Grosvenor Square commemorating Allied Forces who served
in the Burma Campaign and South East Asia Command in the Second World War.

Statue of Lord Mountbatten, the Earl Mountbatten of Burma,
stands close to the Burma memorial in Grosvenor Square.

Evening traffic passing through Dorset Street leaves trails of lights. In the background one of Southampton's newest hotels, Jury's Inn, has been built in the centre of a roundabout!

The mature trees of Lime Avenue were planted in 1862; these line the path due
south through Andrews, Palmerston and Houndwell Parks all the way to Hanover Buildings.

Many pedestrians pass through leafy Andrews Park on their daily commute to work.

Tablet in Andrews Park commemorating Sir Frederick Perkins who, as Mayor, presented this avenue of trees to the town in 1862.

Vibrant flowers in Watts Park. In the background, small shops and pubs line Above Bar Street.

Originally opened in 1928 as the Empire Theatre, this venue has undergone several transformations and many mixed fortunes before finally achieving resounding success under its current name The Mayflower. It is now ranked as one of the three most successful regional theatres in the United Kingdom.

Operating three trains to London Waterloo every hour, Southampton Central Railway Station is a hub of activity night and day.

The BBC South Studios are directly opposite the Civic Centre in Havelock Road.

Skandia House in Portland Terrace is the UK headquarters of Skandia,
a multi-national insurance and investment organisation.

Contemporary sculpture in Havelock Road, with Skandia House in the background.

Modern sculpture in Havelock Road, looking towards the Marlands Shopping Centre.

Unique sculpture in front of the Civic Centre clock tower in Havelock Road.

Southampton's parks are at close proximity to its shopping areas. Here Palmerston Park runs alongside Above Bar Street.

This building with medieval origins has been a public house since 1494, when it was also the old town's first brewing house. Its name was changed to the Duke of Wellington in 1815 to celebrate the famous victory at the Battle of Waterloo.

The Dolphin Hotel on the High Street first opened as an inn in 1506 and has undergone several structural transformations over the years, most notably in the eighteenth century when converted to a coaching inn. It has accommodated many famous historical figures throughout the years, from Lord Nelson, Jane Austen to Queen Victoria.

The Ferryman & Firkin is a popular live music pub next to Holy Rood Church on the High Street.

Statue in one of the city's smaller parks,
Queen's Park near Oxford Street.

Right:
The old Admiralty building in Platform Road was once the General
Post Office, the main post office for Southampton Docks. 1300 bags
of mail that sailed on the *Titanic* would have passed through here.
The building has now been converted into modern apartments.

Like many other prominent buildings near the Docks, South Western House has now been converted into luxury apartments.

Left:
South Western House was once a luxury hotel in which first class transatlantic liner passengers would stay before sailing to New York. Many of the richest people on board the *Titanic* stayed at this hotel before the ship departed on its ill-fated voyage.

Dining al-fresco in one of the many restaurants along Oxford Street.

Now enjoying life as a casino, this building was previously Southampton Terminus Station, and was the main railway station for Southampton Docks. Many first class transatlantic liner passengers would arrive into this station from London before checking into South Western Hotel next door.

The Grapes is a historic pub in Oxford Street which is closely linked with the *Titanic* story as many of the ships crew frequented the pub. One story recounts two crew members, the Slade brothers, who missed the departure of the *Titanic* as they were drinking in The Grapes. As they rushed towards the docks, they inadvertently held up a passenger train full of wealthy passengers also bound for the *Titanic*. Thanks to this bizarre twist of fate, the Slade brothers and train passengers all missed the voyage.

Like many of the older pubs in the city, The Grapes is a living piece of Southampton's history with many stories to tell.

St Mary's Stadium has been the modern home of Southampton Football Club since 2001.
It is a spectacular 32,000 capacity stadium, making it the largest football stadium
in the South of England (outside London).

When Southampton FC moved to the St Mary's Stadium, many fans saw the move as a spiritual homecoming. It was at St Mary's that the club was founded in 1885, when the players were members of the St Mary's Church of England Young Men's Association. Pictured here in the distance is St Mary's Church.

A familiar site to all entering Southampton from Northam Road, the huge gas cylinder towers of Britannia Road gasworks are now giants of a bygone age.

Opened in 1977 the Itchen Bridge connects Woolston with the city centre. The bridge is 870 yards in length, and 92 yards in height at its tallest point.

As the Itchen Bridge cost around £12m to build, a toll system was introduced to recoup the debt. The payback was achieved some years ago, but the toll remains to control traffic in the areas surrounding the bridge.

The Itchen Bridge viewed from Ocean Village.

Due to fire, rebuilding and wartime bombing St Mary's Church has been rebuilt on six occasions. It is considered the mother church of Southampton, despite being outside the original walls of the old town.

Right:
Walkers wander along tree lined paths beside The Avenue.

Below:
Coronation Avenue is a pathway running through Southampton Common, a designated Site of Special Scientific Interest due it its large variety of wildlife.

Although no bodies were returned, there are 45 headstones at Southampton Old Cemetery to victims of the *Titanic* disaster. Pictured is the headstone of one of the *Titanic's* firemen, Harry James Smither.

The grave of Frederick Fleet in Hollybrook Cemetery. Frederick Fleet was the *Titanic* Lookout, the first to notice the fatal iceberg. He survived the disaster and lived until 1965, for a time selling *Echo* newspapers on Pound Tree Road.

Modern art sculptures on the Highfield Campus of the University of Southampton.

The University of Southampton is a highly respected British university which attracts students from all over the world. It was originally formed as the Hartley Institute in 1862.

Above:
State of the art building on Southampton
University's Highfield Campus.

Right:
Southampton University Highfield
Campus along Burgess Road.

The huge Solent Flour Mills building stands behind Gate No.10,
one of the main entrances to Southampton Docks, off West Quay Road.

Closer inspection of the Docks' entrance gate and clock, minus the hands!

The Port of Southampton is home to the UK's second largest container terminal.

Left:
Its position on the opposite side of Southampton Water makes Hythe the ideal place to view the cruise ships in all their glory. In this image, two yachts are dwarfed by the gigantic *Queen Mary 2*.

Below:
Southampton has for long been the departure point for transatlantic liners and is now benefiting from a huge resurgence in the popularity of cruising. Pictured here is a section of the *Queen Mary 2*, the largest and most luxurious ship in the Cunard line.

To get a closer inspection of the great cruise ships, take a trip on the Hythe ferry, which runs regular crossings to Southampton.

Bunting decorating Hythe village centre.

Left:
Southampton Water and the nearby Solent are
extremely popular and busy shipping lanes for passenger,
freight, military and recreational vessels.

Maritime beacon on Hythe waterfront.

Right:
The *QE2* slips silently past Calshot on a summer's dawn,
and enters Southampton Water bound for her home port.

Eighteenth century cottages at Bucklers Hard in the New Forest, a picturesque village located on the banks of the Beaulieu River. Using timber from the New Forest, many Royal Navy warships were built here, including ships in Admiral Nelson's fleet.

The pretty village of Beaulieu in the New Forest was once the site of a Cistercian abbey.
After the Dissolution of the Monasteries, the abbey was mostly destroyed. The gatehouse,
known as Palace House, and abbey ruins are open to the public

Yachts moored in the peaceful
sheltered waters of Lymington marina.

Right:
Yachts safely moored at Eling Quay near Totton.

Cargo ships being
loaded at Southampton
Container Port, viewed
from across the
River Test at Eling shore.

The huge cranes at Southampton Container Port tower high above the stacked containers.

Sunrise at Eling shore, and low tide on the River Test limits activity in the docks.

Fallow deer have grazed the New Forest for nearly 1000 years since being introduced to England by the Normans. They are the most popular deer in the Forest, with an estimated population of around 1500.

The New Forest is synonymous with free roaming ponies. Along with cows, sheep, donkeys and occasionally pigs, the New Forest Ponies graze freely throughout areas of the national park.

A heavy layer of frost sugar coats the heather and bracken
growing on the New Forest heathland near Bolderwood.

As late spring turns to early summer the newly sprouting bracken fronds add a
splash of vibrant green to the New Forest heathland carpet.

Left:
The New Forest has many coniferous woods like this one in the Knightwood Inclosure. While maybe not as romantic
as an ancient oak wood, these pine inclosures can be extremely atmospheric when visited on a misty morning.

Rufus Stone commemorates the location at which
King William the Second died after being struck by
an arrow while hunting in the New Forest.

Left:
Traditional thatched cottages at
Swan Green in the New Forest.

In the graveyard of Pear Tree Church, near Woolston, lies the grave of Richard Parker. Richard was cabin boy aboard the ship *Mignonette* which sank in the South Atlantic during a storm in 1884. The crew of four survived the storm and sinking only to be cast adrift with few provisions in an open boat in the middle of the ocean. Richard's story became a famous and gruesome court case in Victorian England, after it came to light that he was killed and his body eaten by his fellow shipmates.

The ruins of Netley Abbey, a former Cistercian monastery near the town of Netley. After the Dissolution of the Monasteries, the abbey was converted into a mansion by a Tudor politician named William Paulet. It was finally abandoned in the eighteenth century; but its ruined remains have been preserved by English Heritage and are open to the public.

The east window of the ruined church at Netley Abbey.

Boats moored at Swanwick marina in Bursledon.

Low tide at dawn on the River Hamble, near the Bugle pub.

An impressive display of white masts and reflections on the River Hamble at Bursledon.

Bursledon Windmill was built between 1813–14 by Mrs Phoebe Langtry, and is the second windmill to stand upon this site. It was worked until the 1880s, and has recently been renovated and opened to the public.

A model Spitfire is on permanent display outside the entrance to Southampton Airport in Eastleigh. Closely linked with Southampton, the Supermarine Spitfire was designed in the city, and had its first test flight at Eastleigh Airport.